Barry
in old picture postcards

by Tom Clemett

European Library ZALTBOMMEL / THE NETHERLANDS

Cover picture:

Engraving showing Barry Docks in the 1890's, printed and published in

Saxony.

GB ISBN 90 288 1256 3

© 1998 European Library – Zaltbommel/The Netherlands

Introduction

Although not born in Barry, I was brought up in the town, received most of my education there in Cadoxton and Barry Grammar Schools and with this book have tried to recapture in pictures some of the memories I have of the town before so many changes took place.

Cadoxton, where I grew up, has changed completely from open fields, where any time after school or in the holidays you could swim, or in the season wander around picking mushrooms, nuts and blackberries or hide purse nets and a ferret in your pockets and slip out and catch a couple of rabbits as a cheap meal for the family. Most farmers knew what you were up to, but turned a blind eye. Now it's nearly all Chemical Works or housing.

Barry Docks, full of ships and dock workers walking or cycling to work or when coming home from work pouring out of the tunnels at Barry, Barry Docks or Cadoxton; it seemed as though everyone in Barry worked on the docks and finished at the same time.

Barry Dock Town, where shops were owned by the person serving you, where nothing was too much trouble for them, sugar was packed in blue paper cones, cheese cut off to the weight you wanted plus a makeweight which you usually ate on the way home, where every corner had a shop with a book and a choice of three cinemas in town

and two at Cadoxton which you could visit.

Barry Island beach on Miners Holiday Weeks, when the weather was fine, looked like an ant's nest into which somebody had poked a stick, with queues for trays for the sands, queues for fish'n'chips, and queues for the shows on the fairground, but the largest queue of all was for the Scenic Railway, a Barry Island landmark in more ways than one; then finally when it was time to go home, there was another queue for the train.

Porthkerry Park and Romilly Park were an oasis of tranquillity except at Carnival times or when the Barry Horse and Horticultural Shows or the Scouts Fetes were held there.

The Knap, with its swimming pool and boating lake, Bindles Ballroom and the Pebble Beach: these were always considered to be for the residents of Barry, it was often said that 'Barry Island was for Trippers but the Knap was for us'.

I hope that this book will bring back memories of the good times we had, when there seemed to be better summers, with more time to do the things that nowadays we put off and never seem to get round to doing.

Acknowledgements

In compiling this book of photographs of old Barry I have endeavoured to use only photographs from my collection that have not appeared in any other publication. Descriptions of the pictures that are used are mainly from recollections of conversations that I have had with a number of old residents of the town, who on seeing a photograph that I had acquired would usually say 'That's so-and-so' or 'I remember when…' Numbered among these are Jack Stevens and Iorwerth Prothero, both of whom I considered to be friends, and who have sadly passed away. Thanks are also due to Brian Luxton for his books 'Old Barry in Photographs' which I often use to jog my memory, and the staff of the reference rooms at Barry Library for their patience with me whilst looking for confirmation of descriptions or details in the old local newspapers that they have on file; lastly but not least my aunt, Mahala Sayers, for starting me off on local history with her book about our family entitled 'Natters'.

Tom Clemett

1　Old Village Church, Ca-
doxton, in early 1920 with
a wedding taking place,
children at the church
gate, sometimes with a
ribbon held across it waiting for the bride and
groom to appear. Custom
was for a bridal party to
throw coins to the children
to allow them to pass.

2   Another view of the Old Village showing the church and the Three Bells Inn at about the same date as the previous picture. The area in the front of the church is fenced; during the war years a static water tank was built on the area. Thomas Wheelwrights yard stacked with wheels is on the right, Leys Farm in the background has had its thatched roof replaced with a slate one.

The Old Village and Church, Cadoxton.

3 Bridge Street looking towards the King Billy; Hatch Cottage on the right of the picture was partially demolished to allow the road to be widened, the old bridge which gave its name to the street was also demolished. In the foreground the building on the top left is the Sion Calvinistic Church, which was demolished for an extension to Daisy Cottage to be built.

Bridge St Old Cadoxton

4 Cadoxton Court, built on the site of a 15th-century mansion, was renovated in the 19th century for the Rev. John Hughes and later purchased by Mr. Llewellyn, who ran a local newspaper, the Barry & District News, for over forty years. It is now the home of Drs. Bryn and Mary Lennox.

THE COURT, CADOXTON-BARRY.

5 This thirteenth century dovecot in Cadoxton Court is one of only nine left in Glamorgan and is reputed to have had a tunnel underneath it leading to the sea, which at one time came up as far as Weston Square.

THE DOVECOTE
THE COURT, CADOXTON-BARRY.

6 Barry Dock, a favourite view of Barry photographers is this one taken from the Square showing Holton Road in 1911. It must have been a very sunny day when it was taken, as all the shops on the right of the photo have their sun blinds pulled down.

Holton Road, Barry Dock.

7   Holton Road from Evans Street, Cash & Co. have moved from Tynewydd Road to next door, to what is now Lloyds chemist. On the left of the photo James Jones, undertakers, is next to Rees chemist, and Johnson Bros., cleaners and dyers, are on the corner of Richard Street. On the opposite corner is the YWCA.

Holton Road, Barry Docks.

8 Victoria Hotel (now demolished) showing the frontage of the building level with the rest of the properties on the street; this frontage was later demolished and moved back to allow less steep steps to be built, which would be less dangerous for clients entering and leaving the premises after a few drinks. Beynons sweet factory is opposite and Boyles shoe shop is on the corner of Evans Street. Two doors up is Nesbitt, photographers, whose studio was later used by Chas. Farmer up until the 1960's.

Holton Road, Barry Dock.

9   Professor Lloyds Shooting Saloon is on the top of Thompson Street. The brake loaded with passengers is on its way from Barry to the Square. On the right of the photo is Masters, outfitters, with a child in an ornate pram waiting outside. On the opposite corner is Michaelsons, pawnbrokers.

BARRY DOCKS.   Holton Road.

10 Barry Accident and Surgical Hospital opened in 1908. The hospital was built with a south-facing verandah with opening windows to allow patients who were recovering from surgery there, to enjoy the sea breezes and to watch tennis and bowls matches taking place in Central Park. In the First World War it played a major role in treating wounded service-men.

HOSPITAL, BARRY.

11 Another hospital which cared for wounded servicemen was at St. John's Church on Barry Island, run by the nurses of the Voluntary Aid Detachment. Nearly 4,000 bed patients and over 3,000 outpatients were treated there. Its superintendent was Mrs. Pardoe with Drs. Budge and Rees in attendance.

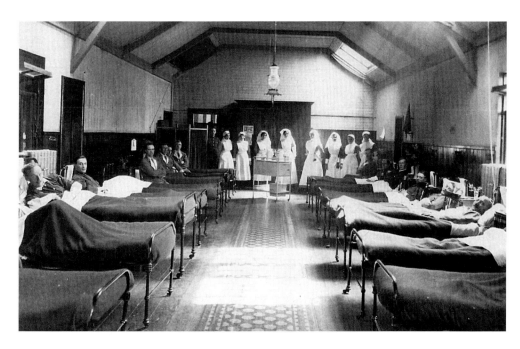

12 Royal Victoria Jubilee Nursing Home, Woodland Road, built with contributions from the residents of Barry to mark the Jubilee of Queen Victoria. Opened in 1899, it was extended in 1904. It became a nurses' residential home on the opening of Barry Accident Hospital, which was later converted into a maternity hospital and is now an adult training and residential centre.

13 The new public offices for Barry Urban District Council were opened by W. J. Williams, J.P. on Wednesday, 22nd April 1908. The photo shows the staff waiting outside for the official opening, together with photographers and curious onlookers.

14 Town Hall, Library and King Square in the early 1950's. There were telephone kiosks outside the Town Hall and floodlights fitted along the front of the building to illuminate it at night. In those days the Borough Council were proud of the Town Hall and liked to show it off to its many admirers.

TOWN HALL, BARRY DOCK

W4633

15   Barry Dock Hotel opened in 1891 as Culleys Hotel and Restaurant, with free drinks for all customers. The hotel was extended twice in its lifetime by the addition of further rooms. The sidebar used by seamen and dockers was known the world over as the 'Chain Locker' and was immortalised by Alexander Cordell in his book 'Rogues March'. The building was demolished in 1983 and Phillipa Freeth Court was built there.

CULLEYS HOTEL. BARRY DOCK

16 Thompson Street was named after a director of the Barry Railway Co. and was reputed to be Barry's answer to Cardiff's Tiger Bay. It was the home of the Sailors' Rest, Liberal, Coronation and RAOB Clubs. There were many cafés and restaurants in the street. As trade at the docks declined many of the buildings fell into disrepair and in the 1970's the street was demolished, destroying a community.

Thompson Street, Barry Docks.

17 Thompson Street from the Dock View Road. The building on the right of the photo is Lloyds Bank showing its impressive frontage. On the opposite side of the street are Freedman's and Hopkin Bros., both maritime outfitters and clothiers vying for trade. Further up the street is a shop owned by Foscolo's, a well-known Barry family, with a hand cart parked outside.

Thompson Street, Barry Docks.

18   Broad Street with the Theatre Royal in the background which was built in 1910 and which offered the public variety, comedy, drama and picture shows. It was used by local amateur dramatic companies to stage their productions. The roof garden on the side of the theatre was to enable patrons to enjoy refreshments between acts. The theatre's musical director was Victor Sylvester, later to be known worldwide for his Ballroom Orchestra.

Broad Street, Barry Docks, showing Theatre.

19 Drill Hall at the bottom of Gladstone Road was opened in 1913 and was used by the T.A. for a great many years. Known by servicemen and its members as 'The Bomb and Dagger' it was always good for a late drink. When T.A. moved its training headquarters to Cardiff, it was sold to Glamorgan College and used as a Performing Arts Studio. On the disposal of college property it was sold and is now used as a funeral home.

20   Memorial Hall, built by public subscription to commemorate the dead of the First World War, was opened in 1932. Designed by Major Hinchsliff, Borough Surveyor, in a classical style, it is one of the most impressive buildings left in Barry. Over 20,000 people attended the opening service.

Memorial Hall & Terraces (1) Barry Dock. 826.

21 Another view of the hall showing the cenotaph, which is now partially obscured by trees planted around it at the time of its building. Over the years the hall has undergone considerable alterations with the building of the Annexe and Town Council Offices.

Memorial Hall & Cenotaph, Barry.

22 Glamorgan Training College opened in 1914 and was extended at a cost of over £50,000 in 1931, 1932 and again after the Second World War. In 1959 the old Barry Grammar School was incorporated into the college and by 1964 the final enlargement took place. On re-organisation of local government the college was sold off to developers, who have since built residential accommodation on the site.

THE COLLEGE, BARRY.

23 Aerial view of Glamorgan Training College before the extensions of 1950. In the background open fields are at the rear of Colcot Road, where the College of Education and Cwm Talwg are now. Very little housing development had taken place on the Buttrills Estate, which at the time the photo was taken still had prefabs on it.

GLAMORGAN TRAINING COLLEGE, BARRY.

24 GWR engine No. 261 standing outside the engine sheds together with other engines, whose bunkers have been refuelled with coal ready for work. No. 261 was a former Barry Railway Co. engine.

25 Barry Dock Offices, built by James Allan and Sons of Cardiff, opened in 1900. Erected in front of the building is one of two statues by Alfred Gilbert, in memory of David Davies, one of the main promoters of the building of the Docks. A replica statue is situated at one of David Davies' earlier construction contracts at Llandinam, the home of the Davies family.

General Offices, Barry Railway & Docks. 1033.

26 SS Hellenic Prince
after repairs at Bailey's Dry
Dock. The ship was used to
carry Jewish refugees from
Europe to Israel after the
Second World War and
whilst engaged in this task
was sabotaged by arsonists.

27 SS Stancliffe undergoing repairs in Bailey's Dry Dock. The ship ran aground at Sharpness and broke in two; it was declared a total loss and sold. Later it was towed to Barry for repair and the two sections were rejoined. In 1948 repairs to the ship were completed and she was renamed SS Gripfast and sold. The Panama Shipping Co. purchased her in 1960, and in the late 1960's she was lost at sea.

28 In September 1935 the French Schooner Goéland loaded with onions coming from France was driven up the Channel in a violent storm and ran ashore on Friars Point. Its cargo was washed ashore and was greatly appreciated by the locals. Just before she struck, the Barry lifeboat Prince David arrived on the scene and with great courage managed to rescue all the crew. In May the following year they were presented with medals from the R.N.L.I. in recognition of their bravery by HRH The Duke of Kent.

29 Advertising card from Ranks Mill. The mill was built in 1905 by Turner Bros. of Cardiff. As an incentive for a mill to be opened in Barry, Ranks were given a long lease at a low rental from the Barry Railway Co. In the 1920's and 1930's cotton flour bags were much sought after by parents of young children to make knickers and petticoats from. The only drawback was the slogan printed on them: 'As You Like It.'

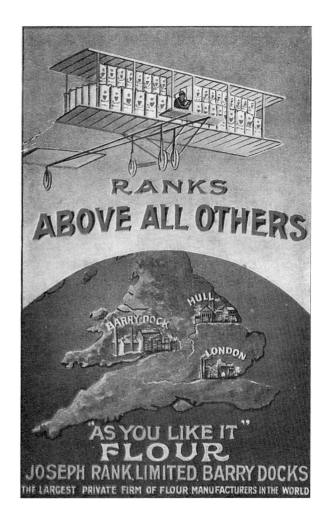

30 Pamir, one of two ships that sailed from Australia carrying grain to Barry. On arrival they were unable to unload their cargo and were moored at Penarth Docks. When they finally arrived in Barry and the hatches were removed a sea of rats was exposed, over 50,000 rats were killed as the grain was unloaded. Pamir later became a cadet sail training ship and in September 1957, outward bound from Buenos Aires, was lost with only six survivors out of a crew of eighty-six, most of whom were cadets.

31 Lily Pads on Tomedge Pond during the Second World War. They were to be used at Normandy as a temporary road surface to unload vehicles straight off the ships, allowing them to be driven ashore; the surface could also be used as a temporary airstrip for light aircraft if needed.

32   Entrance to Barry Docks with Barry Yacht Club craft moored in the harbour. The cabin on the Breakwater railway line is used by Yacht Club race officers to start and finish races by means of a signal gun and the hoisting and lowering of signal flags.

HARBOUR AND DOCK ENTRANCE. BARRY ISLAND.

33 Aerial view of Barry Harbour showing Breakwater and Jacksons Bay with P. & A. Campbells steamer coming in to the landing pontoon. On the right of the photo are the dock entrance and the Lady Windsor Lock; in Bailey's Dry Dock a ship is undergoing repairs.

ENTRANCE TO BARRY HARBOUR

34 Breakwater from the top of Jackson's Bay. On the end of Breakwater is a small beacon built by Chance Bros. It emits a white flashing light, on the other side of the entrance a beacon emitting a red light is situated. These lights act as a guide for shipping entering the docks.

Jacksons Bay & Dock Entrance, Barry Island.

23966

35   Garden Suburb in the 1920's with the signpost indicating Porth-y-Castell, land acquired by Welsh Town Planning and Housing Trust from both the Castle and Cold Knap Farms to build houses to rent. The first phase of development was completed by 1919. Remaining plots were sold to Barry Railway Co. for houses to be built for its employees.

Garden Suburb, Barry

36/37 This panoramic view of the Old Village was taken in 1901. The cottage on the far left is Jordans cottage, which was built as two cottages by the Jones Estate in the early 1800's. The remainder of the cottages were built by Romilly Estate for its workers in the 1860's. The Tudor style building on the far right of the picture is one of the earliest shops in Barry, built in 1865 and owned by Mrs. Green. Her daughter married Mr. C. J. Vaughan, who expanded the business after successfully applying for a licence to sell intoxicants and…

…he became one of Barry's most successful wine and spirit merchants. In 1954 the business was sold to Mr. and Mrs. Williams and in 1959 to Arthur Cooper. It is now owned by Threshers. This card was sent to Australia, was seen in a shop there and sent back to Barry.

38 Another view of the Suburb. The builders' van on the road belongs to Martin Bros. Houses that were built on the Suburb were laid out as required by the Garden City Movement, i.e., twelve houses to the acre.

Garden Suburb, Barry.

39　High Street School was built in 1888 when Walkers School in Queen Street became too small for the number of pupils wanting to attend. When built it was known as the Barry School and its first headmaster was Mr. Whitehouse. It catered for 468 boys, 180 infants and 68 temporary pupils.

HIGH STREET SCHOOLS. BARRY

40 High Street from Trinity Street in 1912. Children are seen outside Griffiths sweet shop and tobacconist; Maynes ironmongery sign is hanging outside No. 109. A bread van is crossing East Street where Woodhams greengrocers and fishmongers shop is open for business

41 Gorsedd stones at the top of Romilly Park, also known as The Druids Circle. It was erected in the 1920's when the Eisteddfod came to Barry for the first time; over the years some of the stones have been removed. The row of houses in the photo are those of the Grove.

Druids' Circle, Barry. 1357.

42   Romilly Park in the 1920's with the bandstand on the far left. The layout of the park has just been completed with flower beds, stone steps and small retaining walls. A very young monkey puzzle tree is in the centre of the flower bed.

Romilly Park, Barry. 1356.

43 Romilly Park, containing over 23 acres, was purchased by Barry Urban District Council at a figure less than its true value from the Romilly Estate in 1898. The shell from the First World War in the foreground was removed for its scrap value prior to the Second World War, as was the tank situated in the triangle at the entrance to the park.

Romilly Park, Barry.

44 Tennis Courts in the park in 1932. The monkey puzzle tree has grown in height and a lot of the trees that surrounded the outside of the park have been cut down to allow for further housing development. The Romilly Estate placed a restrictive covenant on the felling of the trees in the park.

Tennis Courts, Romilly Park, Barry.

45 Aerial view of Porthkerry Park showing the viaduct and Porthkerry House. A number of the properties in the photo have since been demolished or modernised out of recognition.

46 This path leads from Porthkerry village through the gate and under the viaduct to the beach. The viaduct consists of 16 arches in total; these vary in height from 45 feet to 50 feet, the total height of the structure is over 100 feet.

Porthkerry Park, Barry

47 Steam train emerging from the tunnel on what was the Vale of Glamorgan Railway. The line, although closed to ordinary passenger traffic, is still used to allow trains to carry coal to Aberthaw Power Station and the 125 London-to-Swansea Express to continue to operate when main line working is halted for maintenance.

PORTHKERRY PARK, BARRY.

48 Work on the viaduct started in 1894 and was completed in 1897. In that year it closed owing to the partial collapse of one of its piers. It was re-opened in January 1898. Whilst it was closed a loop line was built around the park to allow the carriage of coal to take still place. The photo was taken in 1923, when cattle and sheep were allowed to roam freely.

Barry, from South Side. Viaduct, Porthkerry Park.   1117

49 Porthkerry Church (St. Curig's), built in the 13th century, contains stained glass windows dedicated to the Savours family of Rhoose. In 1927 an organ was installed in memory of the nine men of the village who fell in the First World War; their names are inscribed on a brass plaque fitted to the side of the instrument. The lych gate at the entrance to the church is also dedicated to their memory.

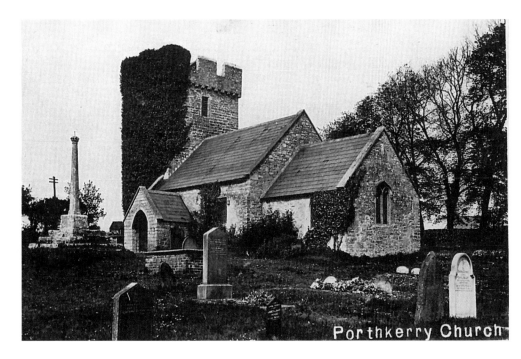

Porthkerry Church

50　St. Nicholas Road is named after the church which was formerly the parish church of Barry. In the background Bethel Baptist Church, built in 1903. Turning on the right of the photo is Canon Street.

Barry. St. Nicholas Road.

51 Cold Knap in 1924 was completely undeveloped, having only a few buildings erected upon it. At the rear of the photo in the centre are the Knap Hotel, Luens café and tea rooms, together with a small number of other properties. The large building is the White House (now demolished).

Cold Knapp, Barry.

52 Knap pool, opened in 1927, was built by unemployed workmen who were paid with vouchers valued 10/- for a week's work; these vouchers could be exchanged at local shops. The picture shows the pool at its opening with ladders placed against the side to enable swimmers to climb out. The ladders were anchored in place by a 56 lb weight tied to foot.

The Swimming Baths, Cold Knap, Barry

53 The pool in the early 1950's. On the right the Knap Hotel which was demolished to enable Sea Point flats to be built on the site. In the background Bindles Ballroom which closed in the 1980's and Glan-y-Mor YMCA Residential Hostel, which opened in 1932 and was demolished to enable the building of houses on the site.

BRY 59   THE BATHING POOL, COLD KNAP, BARRY   A TUCK CARD

54 The pool in the 1950's showing the diving boards in the background and behind them the swimming clubhouse, the first aid hut and the old snack bar. Some days groups of shivering youngsters gripping hot drinks with both hands and trying to stop the contents from slopping over could be seen outside. These buildings were demolished when a new entrance block and The Snacpac were built.

55 Knap Hotel, owned and run by Mrs. Luen, is the large building in a sea of tents belonging to various scout groups who were given permission to hold their annual camp on the site. In the centre of the tents is Sid Luen's tea rooms.

The Walk & Lake, Cold Knap, Barry. 947.

56 Watchtower Bay showing the Breakwater, which over the years has been lowered in height by sand drifting in from the Channel and building up around its base. In the 1950's the Bristol Channel Swimming Race, an annual event organised by Barry Swimming Club, was held in the Bay.

THE OLD HARBOUR, BARRY

W 6129

57   A rowing regatta is taking place in the Old Harbour and Watchtower Bay. Barry Rowing Club, one of the oldest sporting clubs in Barry, regularly ran them there. Cold Knap Farm and the White House built by Sir William Graham are in the background. The house has been demolished and White House development has taken its place.

WATCH HOUSE BAY, BARRY.

40

58 In 1901 a portion of the beach was set aside by the Windsor Estate as a children's play area. In this photo there are only children playing there. Sand dunes are clearly visible in the background, showing that the beach had not been developed when this picture was taken.

The Childrens' Playground, Barry Island.

59 Paddling Pool at Friars Point in 1905. Landing stages for trips around the bay were moved down the beach as the tide went out but were not required near the pool, as the steps on the side could be used to board the boats. The post on the edge of the pool was placed there to show boat operators the location of the pool when the tide was in.

Bathing Pool, Barry Island (1).

60 A family group dressed for the seaside in 1903. The picture shows the pool with boats moored ready to take passengers. Before the development of the fairground, the beach, donkey rides and boat trips were the only attractions on the island. By 1910 other beach attractions included Johnny Shield's group of Pierrots and stage shows in the Old Pavilion, Punch & Judy shows and a small fairground at the eastern end of the beach.

Barry Island from the Rocks.

61 Bathing huts were wheeled down to the water's edge to enable visitors wanting to bathe to enter the water. They were used until the island became so popular that queues formed to use them. So many complaints were received by the council about the time bathers spent waiting to use them, that they allowed visitors to bathe subject to the approval of an inspector of bathing costumes appointed by the council.

Sands, Barry Island.

62 Children in a donkey cart at Friars Road at the eastern end of the half-penny prom. In the background are the sand dunes of Nells Point. In 1910, when this photo was taken by Mr. Howe of Barry, 'sailor boy' suits as worn by the younger members of the Royal Family were fashionable wear for the children of fairly well-off families.

63 The western end of the half-penny prom is shown in this photo. It was opened in 1905 by the Windsor Estate and at first cost 1d to use, which in the first three months of its opening was reduced by half, hence its name. The buildings on the left are the Barry Island Refreshment Rooms and a toilet block (which has since been demolished), complete with its line of 'What the Butler Saw'-machines outside the buildings.

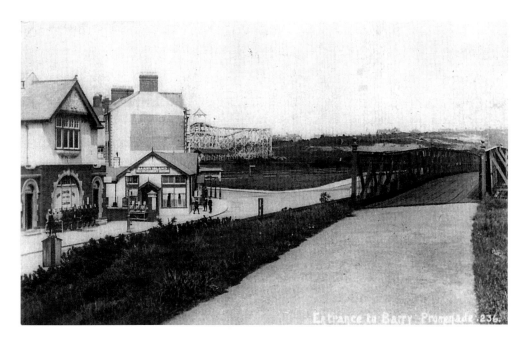

Entrance to Barry Promenade. 236.

64 The coastguard station on Nells Point seen from Redbrink Crescent. Most of the buildings on the point were demolished in the 1960's, when Butlin's Camp was built there. The building on the right of the photo is the Garrison headquarters, used by crews of the gun battery that was stationed there. Tents pitched along the point were used by the T.A. and troops who were sent there for training.

Barry Island, Coast Guard Station.

65 Breakwater Cove in 1905 was renamed Jacksons Bay by locals after the builder of the Breakwater, Sir John Jackson, who was also responsible for the building of the Lady Windsor Lock and the Commercial Dry Dock (Bailey's Dry Dock).

Breakwater Cove, (1) Barry Island

66 Jackson's Bay in 1938, showing that the number of army huts on the point have increased, possibly due to the imminent outbreak of the war, which would have required more soldiers to be stationed there to man the guns, and if needed, to relieve servicemen stationed on Flat Holm.

JACKSONS BAY, BARRY   W.1883

67 Seven pleasure boats can be seen plying for hire in this photo taken in 1920, but there are still visitors waiting to board them. Donkey rides were also very popular, but there are very few bathers in the water.

General View of Barry Island, towards Nell's Point. 1119

68 Pat Collin's fairground in the 1930's. In the centre of the photo is the water chute, with dodgems on the left and a speedway scenic on the right. In the background is Thompson's Figure 8, built in 1912 and replaced in 1939 by the Scenic Railway.

THE PLEASURE PARK, BARRY ISLAND

69   Barry Island in 1934. On August Bank Holiday weekend over 100,000 visitors visited Barry Island; looking at this photo it seems as though most of them are on the beach. In order for them to return home, trains left the station every ten minutes from 6 p.m. until 10 p.m.

70 Barry Island in the 1950's. The Scenic Railway in the background has just received a coat of cement wash. Strato-Globe is at the entrance to the fairground, Crane's fish'n'chips, snack bar and refreshment stall is next to Forte's ice cream parlour, the Roxy Cinema at the end of the Esplanade Buildings (now The Roller-drome) with its non-stop film shows is open for business.

AMUSEMENT PARK AND GARDENS, BARRY ISLAND.

W.3025.

71 The Guinness Clock on the promenade in the 1950's was a tremendous attraction; hundreds of visitors would stand and watch when it was time for the hour to change. After it left Barry it appeared at many different resorts around the country. Its last reported appearance was at Blackpool.

72 Another view of the clock just before the hour is to change. Visitors are starting to gather to watch the actions of the clock.

73 Aerial photo of Barry taken in the late 1920's, showing the Old Harbour and West Pond (now car park). The work on the promenade can still be seen taking place.

AEROFILMS SERIES   AIR VIEW OF BARRY ISLANDS   29458

74 View of Friars Point with Sir William Graham's House (Friars Point Guest House) in the centre. Railway sidings are on what is now the car park, and in the background there are large open spaces where development of Barry has not yet taken place.

AEROFILMS SERIES   FRIARS POINT, BARRY   29459

75   View from Garden Suburb showing the causeway to Barry Island dividing West Pond from the Old Harbour. Romilly Park is the large open space in the right of the photo. From the air Friars Point and the two bays resemble a giant fish.

AEROFILMS SERIES   AIR VIEW OF BARRY & BARRY ISLANDS   29392

76 Nells Point in 1921 with the Garrison and Coastguard Buildings. Forrest Drive can be clearly seen encircling the point, the fairground has not been developed nor has work started on the building of the prom. St. Baruch's Church stands alone halfway down Plymouth Road and can be clearly seen, as housing development has not yet begun.

Whitmore Bay & Barry Docks from the Air.